ISBN: 0801044111

to

_____

from

_____

date

_____

D1497111

N l' Noah's Al Ark

PRECIOUS MOMENTS

Illustrated by Sam Butcher

Baker Books

A Division of Baker Book House Co
Grand Rapids, Michigan 49516

Art © 1979, 1981, 1987, 1996 by Precious Moments, Inc.
Text © 1998 by Baker Book House

Published by Baker Books
a division of Baker Book House Company
P.O. Box 6287, Grand Rapids, MI 49516-6287

Printed in the United States of America

Library of Congress Cataloging-in-Publication Data

Precious Moments Noah's Ark.
          p.   cm.
     Summary: A retelling of the Old Testament story which tells how Noah built a huge ark that kept his family and two of every kind of animal safe during a great flood.
     ISBN 0-8010-4411-1
     1. Noah's ark—Juvenile literature. [1. Noah (Biblical figure) 2. Noah's ark. 3. Bible stories—O.T.] I. Precious Moments, Inc.
BS658.P74   1998
222'.1109505—DC21   98-30869

For current information about all releases from Baker Book House, visit our web site:
http://www.bakerbooks.com

Once, a long time ago, there was a man named Noah. He lived in a big city with many other people. Of all the people in that city, God was most pleased with Noah, because Noah loved God and listened to what he said.

One day God spoke to Noah.

"Noah," God said, "I'm going to send a lot of rain. More rain than you've ever seen before. But don't be afraid. I'll tell you how to build a big boat that will keep you safe from the rain. We'll call this boat an ark, and it will be perfect."

Then God said, "Noah, this ark will be big enough for you and your whole family—and many animals— two of every kind!"

Noah began to build the ark. It took a long time, but Noah didn't give up. Noah's friends laughed at him. But he kept on working. There was no rain in sight. But still Noah worked on and on. And finally the ark was finished.

Then Noah and his family watched as the animals made their way to the ark. Two by two, the animals came from everywhere!

Two goats walked side-by-side over the hills and through the valleys, right up to the big doors of the ark. Together they walked on board.

Two elephants remembered to walk
on board, and they were just in time!
They held their trunks together and,
one step at a time, made their way
onto the ark.

Two zebras raced to the ark. Their stripes zig-zagged in the sun as they hurried along to take their place on the ark.

Two giraffes untied themselves long enough to walk on board. Neck and neck they walked, as fast as their long legs would carry them.

Two lions walked on board looking proud and mighty. They shook their great manes and then curled up and went to sleep.

Two mice walked to the ark, with the help of a friend. Slowly, slowly they moved toward the ark until, at last, they were there!

Two owls flew over the ark and
circled once or twice. At last they
found a perch high up on the top of the
ark, where they could see everything!

And last but not least, two little bunnies hopped on board.

Finally, Noah closed the door of the ark. His family and all the animals were safe inside.

And suddenly it happened. First one drop, then another. Soon rain was pouring from the sky. More rain than Noah had ever seen!

Rain tapped on the roof. Rain beat on the door. It would not stop! The ark sailed on, tossed about on the water. Each day Noah searched the sky, hoping for a ray of sunshine. But each day more rain came. For forty days and forty nights there was rain, nothing but rain!

Then one day Noah heard nothing! No rain tapping on the roof! No rain beating on the door! What could this mean?

Noah rushed to the window and there, to his great surprise, he saw the bright beautiful sun!

Soon Noah and his family could find dry land and leave the ark. The earth was fresh and clean again. And God had kept them safe, just as he had promised.

In God's care Noah knew he would always be safe. God had kept his promise. But he did even more. As a sign of his promise and his love for Noah and his family, God sent something wonderful. No one had ever seen anything like it before. It was a beautiful ribbon of color and it stretched across the sky. It was a rainbow to remind Noah and us that God keeps his promises.

The End